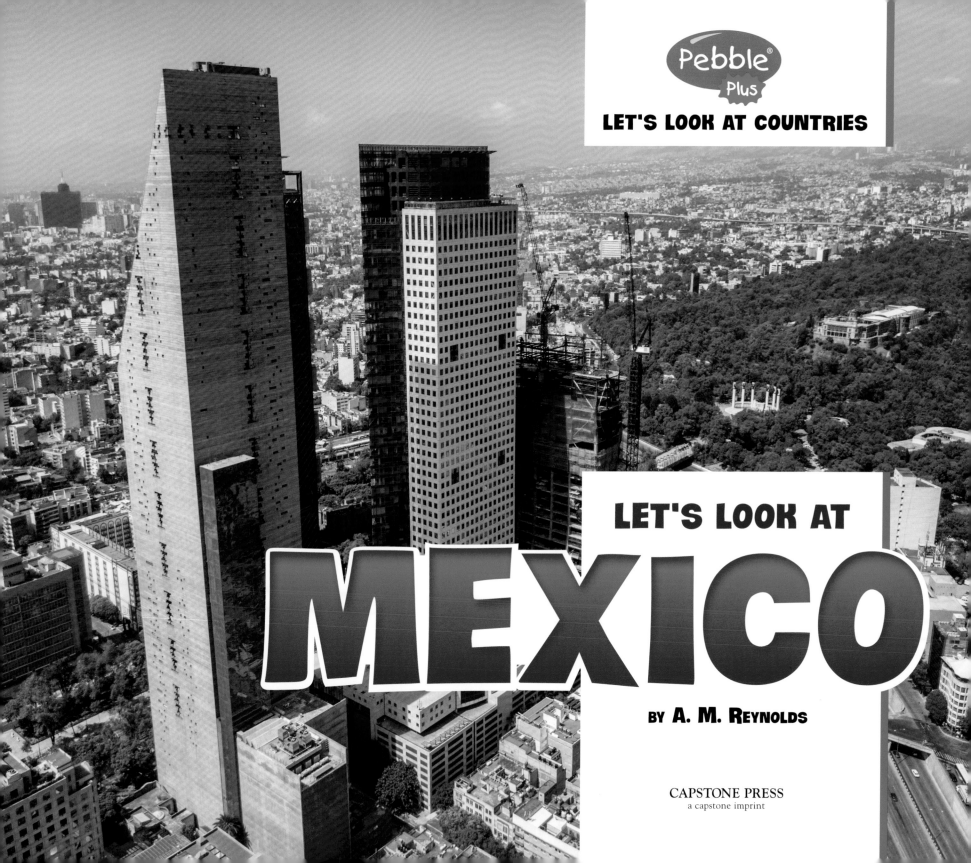

Pebble® Plus

LET'S LOOK AT COUNTRIES

LET'S LOOK AT

MEXICO

BY A. M. REYNOLDS

CAPSTONE PRESS
a capstone imprint

Pebble Plus is published by Capstone Press,
1710 Roe Crest Drive, North Mankato, Minnesota 56003
www.mycapstone.com

**Library of Congress Cataloging-in-Publication Data**
Names: Reynolds, A. M., 1958– author.
Title: Let's look at Mexico / by A.M. Reynolds.
Description: North Mankato, Minnesota : Capstone Press, 2019. | Series: Pebble plus. Let's look at countries
Identifiers: LCCN 2018029938 (print) | LCCN 2018031724 (ebook) | ISBN 9781977103925 (eBook PDF) | ISBN 9781977103833 (hardcover) | ISBN 9781977105622 (pbk.)
Subjects:  LCSH: Mexico—Juvenile literature.
Classification: LCC F1208.5 (ebook) | LCC F1208.5 .R49 2019 (print) | DDC 972—dc23
LC record available at https://lccn.loc.gov/2018029938

**Editorial Credits**
Erika L. Shores, editor; Juliette Peters, designer; Jo Miller, media researcher;
Laura Manthe, production specialist

**Photo Credits**
Shutterstock: Aberu.Go, 1, Aleksandar Todorovic, 17, Anton_Ivanov, 9, 21, Art Konovalov, 19, Chepe Nicoli, Cover Top, EddieHernandezPhotography, 11, Globe Turner, 22 (Inset), IR Stone, Cover Middle, Jakub Zajic, 13, Kobby Dagan, 14, 15, nate, 4, Rafael Ramirez Lee, 22-23, 24, saad315, 8, Simon Dannhauer, 6, stacyarturogi, Cover Bottom, Cover Back, Sven Hansche, 3, THPStock, 7, Ulrike Stein, 5

## Note to Parents and Teachers

The Let's Look at Countries set supports national curriculum standards for social studies related to people, places, and culture. This book describes and illustrates Mexico. The images support early readers in understanding the text. The repetition of words and phrases helps early readers learn new words. This book also introduces early readers to subject-specific vocabulary words, which are defined in the Glossary section. Early readers may need assistance to read some words and to use the Table of Contents, Glossary, Read More, Internet Sites, Critical Thinking Questions, and Index sections of the book.

Printed and bound in China.
970

# TABLE OF CONTENTS

# Where Is Mexico?

Mexico is a country in North America. It is almost three times bigger than the U.S. state of Texas. Mexico's capital is Mexico City.

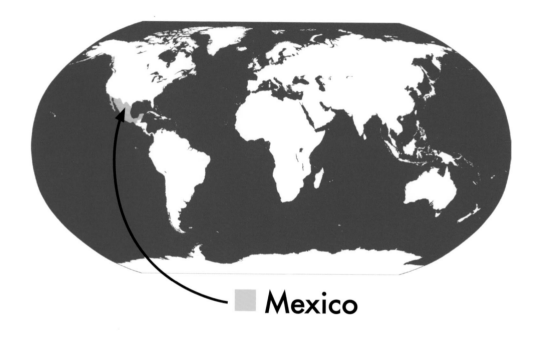

Mexico

Mexico City, Mexico

# From Rain Forests to Deserts

Mexico has mountains, rain forests, canyons, and deserts. Three bodies of water surround Mexico.

The country has many beaches.

# In the Wild

All kinds of animals live in Mexico. Ocelots are wildcats that live in rain forests. Howler monkeys swing from treetops. Gray whales swim in waters around Mexico.

ocelot

howler monkey

# People

Most Mexicans live in cities.

The middle of the country is home

to the most people.

Mexicans speak Spanish.

# At the Table

Mexicans use herbs and vegetables in their food. They eat tacos, enchiladas, and guacamole. The food is full of flavor.

# Festivals

Cities and towns hold fiestas throughout the year. These festivals have parades, fireworks, and mariachi bands with guitars and trumpets.

# On the Job

Most Mexicans work in jobs

that help other people.

They help tourists in hotels

and restaurants. Other people work

at banks, hospitals, or schools.

# Transportation

Mexicans travel in cars and airplanes.

Only the United States and Brazil

have more airports than Mexico.

Many Mexicans ride buses

in the countryside.

# Famous Site

Chichen Itza is an old city in Mexico.

The Mayan people built it

1,500 years ago. It has

a 79-foot (24-meter) high pyramid.

# CK MEXICO FACTS

Mexican flag

**Name:** United Mexican States

**Capital:** Mexico City

**Other major cities:** Guadalajara, Puebla

**Population:** 124,574,795 (2017 estimate)

**Size:** 758,450 square miles (1,964,375 sq km)

**Language:** Spanish

**Money:** Mexican Peso

# GLOSSARY

fiesta—a holiday or festival in Mexico

guacamole—a mashed dip made from avocados

mariachi band—a lively group of musicians with trumpets
and guitars

Mayan—belonging to the ancient civilization of Maya

pyramid—a building with triangular shaped sides and
a point at the top

tourist—someone who travels and visits other places
for fun

# READ MORE

**Blevins, Wiley.** *Mexico.* Follow Me Around. New York: Scholastic, 2018.

**Kopp, Megan.** *Mexico.* Countries. New York: Smartbook Media, Inc., 2017.

**Markovics, Joyce.** *Mexico City.* Citified! New York: Bearport Publishing, 2018.

# INTERNET SITES

Use FactHound to find Internet sites related to this book.

Visit *www.facthound.com*

Just type 9781977103833 and go.

Super-cool stuff!

Check out projects, games and lots more at
www.capstonekids.com

# CRITICAL THINKING QUESTIONS

1. What language is spoken in Mexico?

2. Name two things you might see at a fiesta.

3. What shape are the sides of a pyramid?

# INDEX